follow-up maths 6

money

Paul Briten

Contents

© Oxford University Press 1979

The value of money

1. Which of these coins are silver?
2. Which coins are bronze?
3. Write the coins in order of value: $\frac{1}{2}$p; _ _ _ _ _.
4. Name 3 objects which might cost: a $\frac{1}{2}$p b 1p c 2p d 5p
   e 10p f 50p.

5. Which 2 coins will exactly pay for each of these items:

6. Which 3 coins could you use to pay exactly for these:

2

Counting quickly

When counting coins it is easier if you count the highest values first.

$$50p + 10p + 10p + 5p + 2p + 1p + 1p + \tfrac{1}{2}p = 79\tfrac{1}{2}p$$

1. How much money is in each of these boxes?

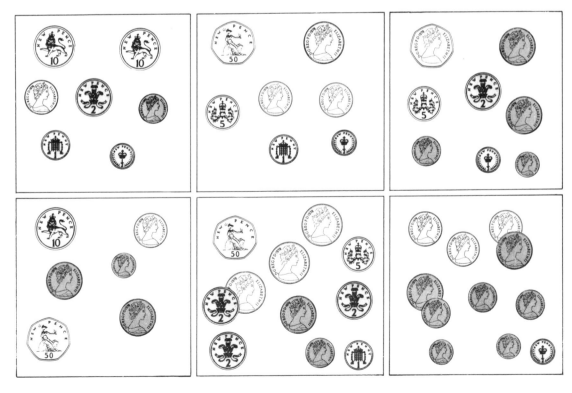

Pound for pound

1. A one pound note has the same value as :

   two 50 p coins
   a ☐ 10 p coins
   b ☐ 5 p coins
   c ☐ 2 p coins
   d ☐ 1 p coins
   e ☐ ½ p coins

2. Add up the coins below to decide who has the most money :

CINDERELLA

BASHER

ELEPHANT TRAINER

MRS. MONEYPENNY

The right change

1. Copy and complete this table.

	Amount of money	Number of coins	Value of each coin
	15p	four	10p 2p 2p 1p
a	$12\frac{1}{2}$p	three	— — —
b	27p	four	— — — —
c	59p	six	— — — — — $\frac{1}{2}$p
d	5p	nine	— — — — — — — — —
e	$80\frac{1}{2}$p	six	— — — — —
f	35p	five	— — — —
g	44p	six	— — — — —
h	98p	eight	— — — — — — —
i	72p	seven	— — — 5p — — $\frac{1}{2}$p
j	54p	five	— — — — $\frac{1}{2}$p
k	18p	four	— — — —
l	50p	eight	— — — — — — 2p —

2. From this display which two items can you buy for **exactly**:

a 13p   b 33p   c 25p
d 6p   e 22p   f 28p
g 23p   h 30p   i 21p

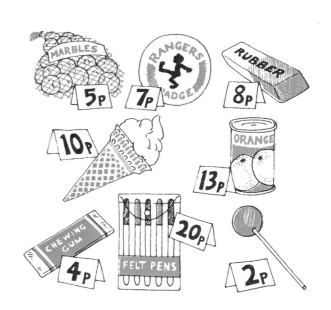

Which 3 different items can you buy for **exactly**:

a 33p   b 21p   c 11p
d 43p   e 34p   f 24p

Changing pennies

$$100p = £1 \qquad\qquad 1p = \tfrac{1}{100} \text{ of } £1$$

Pennies can be written as decimal fractions of £1.

$1p = £0·01 \qquad\qquad 2p = £0·02 \qquad\qquad 5p = £0·05$

$10p = £0·10 = \tfrac{1}{10} \text{ of } £1 \qquad\qquad 13p = £0·13$

The 2 figures after the decimal point show the number of pennies.

$£1·16p \times$

Never write the '£' and 'p' signs together. $£1·16 \checkmark$

1. Write these amounts as decimal fractions of £1.

a 8p	b 4p	c 9p	d 15p	e 19p	f 27p
g 49p	h 82p	i 52p	j 41p	k 68p	l 70p
m 85p	n 96p	o 32p	p 77p	q 18p	r 3p

2. 120p is written as £1·20

   Write these amounts in pounds:

a 110p	b 158p	c 187p	d 256p	e 321p
f 497p	g 826p	h 722p	i 961p	j 276p

3. When halfpennies are written, they are added at the end of the decimal fraction:

   $$1\tfrac{1}{2}p = £0·01\tfrac{1}{2} \qquad\qquad 7\tfrac{1}{2}p = £0·07\tfrac{1}{2}$$

   Write these amounts in pounds:

a $9\tfrac{1}{2}$p	b $6\tfrac{1}{2}$p	c $15\tfrac{1}{2}$p	d $22\tfrac{1}{2}$p	e $41\tfrac{1}{2}$p
f $79\tfrac{1}{2}$p	g $99\tfrac{1}{2}$p	h $118\tfrac{1}{2}$p	i $127\tfrac{1}{2}$p	j $226\tfrac{1}{2}$p

Lost in a supermarket

58p + 24p + £1·07 = ☐
When you are adding money the
following method will help you:

			£
		58p	0·58
58p + 24p + £1·07	is the same as	24p is the same as	0·24
		+£1·07	+1·07
			£1·89

Follow the correct total of each bill below to find out which door
is the exit:

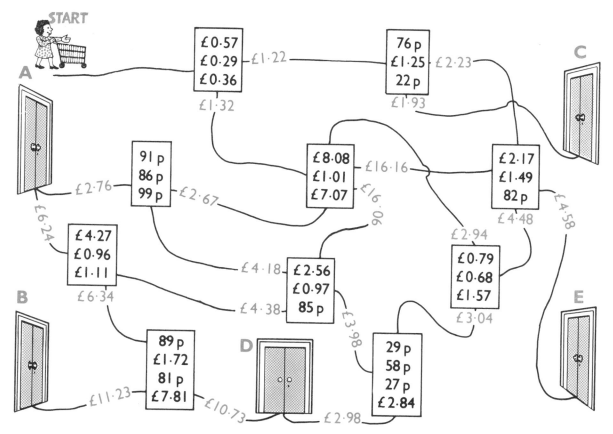

Check up 1

1. Copy and complete this table:

	Amount	Number of coins	Coins
	22 p	3	10p 10p 2p
a	17 p	3	
b	48 p	7	
c	25 p	3	
d	81 p	5	
e	$26\frac{1}{2}$ p	5	
f	$99\frac{1}{2}$ p	9	
g	66 p	4	
h	£1·10	3	
i	£1·79	8	

2. Add these groups of coins:

a 10p   10p   2p $\frac{1}{2}$p
b 50p   5p   2p   1p   1p $\frac{1}{2}$p
c 10p   10p   5p   5p   50p
d 2p   2p   10p $\frac{1}{2}$p   50p
e $\frac{1}{2}$p   10p   50p   50p   10p
f 2p $\frac{1}{2}$p $\frac{1}{2}$p   50p   10p   1p
g 10p   50p $\frac{1}{2}$p   2p   5p
h 10p   2p   5p   10p   1p
i 1p   10p $\frac{1}{2}$p   50p   50p
j 2p   5p   50p $\frac{1}{2}$p   10p

3. Work out the smallest number of coins that could be used to pay for each of these toys:

a 84p b 98p c 64p d $77\frac{1}{2}$p e $88\frac{1}{2}$p f 92p

4. Copy and complete:

	84 p	£0·84	h	116 p	
a	62 p		i	119 p	
b	79 p		j	227 p	
c	48 p		k	314 p	
d	$11\frac{1}{2}$ p		l	426 p	
e	$17\frac{1}{2}$ p		m	$384\frac{1}{2}$ p	
f	$88\frac{1}{2}$ p		n		£1·$99\frac{1}{2}$
g	$92\frac{1}{2}$ p		o		£8·$51\frac{1}{2}$

The shopkeepers' method

Shopkeepers often use the 'Shopkeepers method' for giving change:

The change shopkeeper gives

As he gives the money he says:

fifty- ~ fifty- ~ sixty ~ seventy ~ eighty ~ ninety ~ one
seven   eight   pound

Total change 43 p.

1. Draw diagrams like the one above to show the change from £1 for these costs:

   a 47 p   b 58 p   c 65 p   d 22 p   e 18 p   f 12 p

2. Copy and complete this table:

	Cost	money given	coins given for change	total change
	45 p	£1	5 p 50 p	55 p
a	24 p	£1		
b	39 p	£1		
c	21 p	50 p		
d	33 p	£1		

Mr Baker's holiday

Mr Baker is taking his family on holiday. On the way he buys petrol and refreshments. Charges are shown in red Money given by Mr Baker is in black.
Follow the route showing correct amounts of change to discover where they are going.

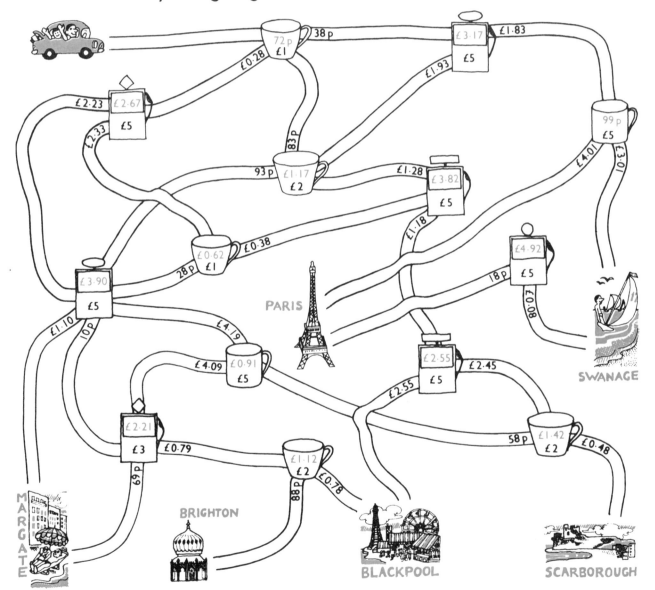

Bills

When you buy several items from a shop, setting out a bill helps you to find the total cost:

	£
book	0·84
game	1·72
ball	+ 0·62½
	3·18½
	⌄2

1. Set out bills for:

   a dartboard and darts
   b skateboard and training shoes
   c kite, darts and ball
   d skateboard and book
   e dartboard, kite and skateboard
   f game, kite, shoes and darts
   g all 8 items

2. Set out and total these amounts:

   a 54p + £1·27 + £2·43
   b 89p + £2·16 + 25p
   c £0·87 + £4 + 98p
   d £0·78 + £3·85
   e £2·27 + £1·86 + £3·21
   f £2·66 + £1·92 + £3·87
   g £4·86 + 94p + £2·91
   h £10·11 + £6·71 + 88p
   i £62·14 + £59·57
   j £107·28 + 24p + £1·79

Crosswords 1

1.

Copy and complete these crosswords by writing the answers in pounds. When an answer is less than £1, write '0' in front of the decimal point.

Across:

4 £1·17 + £1·34	1 85 p + 47 p
8 £2·65 + £1·14	7 84 p + £2·12
10 £0·39 + 29 p	9 £3·33 + £3·41
15 £1·88 + £2·69	13 £3·86 + £3·28
18 £4·87 + £1·79	17 47 p + 49 p
20 £2·15 + £4·87 + £1·95	19 86 p + 37 p

Down:

1 £10·41 + £2·24	2 £2·29 + £1·68	3 £15·78 + £10·69
4 £17·61 + £5·46	5 £1·19 + £4·57	6 £3·99 + £15·85
11 £14·68 + £7·24	12 £4·87 + £10·82	13 £3·68 + £3·33
14 £1·85 + £2·78	15 98 p + £3·70	16 £1·18 + £6·49

2.

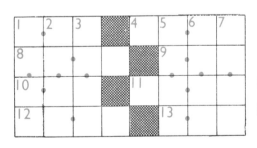

Across:

4 £18·97 + £2·25	1 £1·36 + 75 p
9 £1·17 + £7·23	8 £16·57 + £9·40
11 £19·91 + £7·44	10 64 p + £3·14
13 £2·78 + £1·26 + £2·17	12 £8·76 + £5·89

Down:

1 £17·68 + £4·63	2 £9·87 + £5·87	3 £4·29 + £15·57
5 £4·92 + £13·84	6 £20·07 + £4·25	7 £0·96 + £19·55

Spend, spend, spend

Sam has 75 p. He spends 37 p. How much has he left?
He can find out by adding on:

3p + 10p + 10p + 10p + 5p = 38p

37 p   40 p   50 p   60 p   70 p   75 p

or by setting out the figures
and subtracting

$$\begin{array}{r} £ \ ^6 \\ 0 \cdot 7\ ^15 \\ -0 \cdot 3\ 7 \\ \hline 0 \cdot 3\ 8 \end{array}$$

Jill has £2. She spends 58 p. How much has she left?

2p + 10p + 10p + 10p + 10p + £1

58 p   60 p   70 p   80 p   90 p   £1   £2

$$\begin{array}{r} {}^1£\ ^9 \\ 2 \cdot\ ^10\ ^10 \\ -\quad 5\ 8 \\ \hline 1 \cdot 4\ 2 \end{array}$$

Copy and complete this table:

	Amount	Money spent	Money left (1)	(2)
a	63 p	38 p	2p + 10p + 10p + 3p 38p 40p 50p 60p 63p · 25 p	£ 0·63 −0·38 ———
b	82 p	16 p		
c	£1·00	43 p		
d	£2·00	85 p		
e	£1·76	49 p		
f	£1·20	67 p		

Shopping spree

1. Mr Bone has £5. Follow his trail. He spends 9 p, then £1·35, then 14 p. How much has he left?
2. Follow the trails for each of the other people, and work out how much they have left at the end.

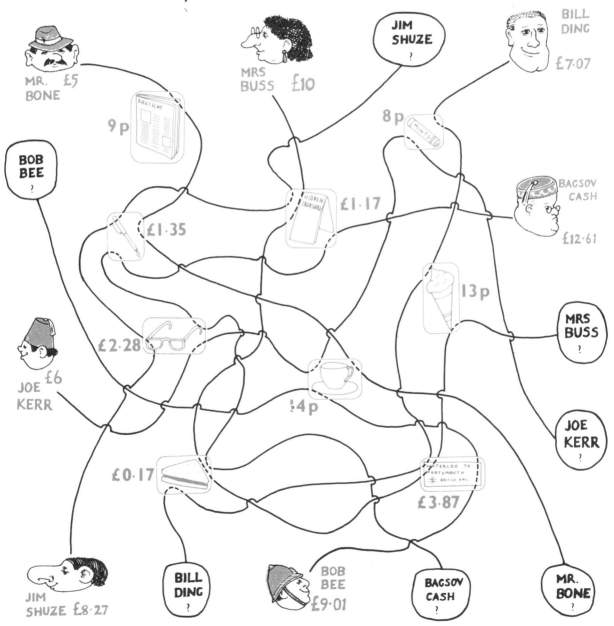

Sum problems

Work out the answers to the following:

1.
a £
   6·13
 + 1·86
 _____

b £
   4·27
 + 2·19
 _____

c £
   5·68
 + 2·96
 _____

d £
   7·16$\frac{1}{2}$
 + 5·89
 _____

e £
   2·48$\frac{1}{2}$
   1·17
 + 3·42$\frac{1}{2}$
 _____

f £
   6·82$\frac{1}{2}$
   4·96$\frac{1}{2}$
 + 5·83$\frac{1}{2}$
 _____

g £
   12·96
   4·85
 + 26·92
 _____

h £
   16·77$\frac{1}{2}$
   41·88$\frac{1}{2}$
 + 90·16
 _____

i £
   4·38
 − 2·16
 _____

j £
   5·91
 − 1·65
 _____

k £
   8·86$\frac{1}{2}$
 − 4·23
 _____

l £
   12·42$\frac{1}{2}$
 − 3·57
 _____

Look at this example:

$$\begin{array}{r} £^{5} \\ 2 \cdot 16 \\ -\ 1 \cdot 02\frac{1}{2} \\ \hline 1 \cdot 13\frac{1}{2} \\ \hline \end{array}$$

2. Now do these:

a £
   4·29
 − 1·18$\frac{1}{2}$
 _____

b £
   3·64
 − 1·48$\frac{1}{2}$
 _____

c £
   9·14
 − 3·78$\frac{1}{2}$
 _____

d £
   17·61
 − 9·96$\frac{1}{2}$
 _____

Check up 2

1. Copy and complete:

	Cost	Money given	Change
	27 p	50 p	23 p
a	69 p	£1	
b	48 p		52 p
c	17 p	£1	
d	$26\frac{1}{2}$ p	£1	
e		£2	86 p
f		60 p	$9\frac{1}{2}$ p
g	£1·69	£5	
h	£1·$18\frac{1}{2}$		$31\frac{1}{2}$
i		£2·00	82 p
j	£2·$27\frac{1}{2}$	£3·00	

2. Copy and complete:

	Amount	Money spent	Money left
	82 p	46 p	36 p
a	57 p	19 p	
b	£1·16	48 p	
c	£1·63		48 p
d		69 p	78 p
e	£2·16	£0·92	
f		£2·72	£1·68
g	£2·$77\frac{1}{2}$		$48\frac{1}{2}$ p
h		$88\frac{1}{2}$ p	£1·$71\frac{1}{2}$

3. Set out and total these amounts:

a 58 p + £1·06
b 39 p + £1·47 + 81 p
c £1·$16\frac{1}{2}$ + £8·$92\frac{1}{2}$
d £2·$79\frac{1}{2}$ + $64\frac{1}{2}$ p + 29 p
e £14·68 + £36·$17\frac{1}{2}$
f £5·74 + £8·$00\frac{1}{2}$
g £61·27 + £14·09 + $85\frac{1}{2}$ p
h £112·68 + £170·02
i £100·60 + £16·$80\frac{1}{2}$
j £27·$27\frac{1}{2}$ + £72·$72\frac{1}{2}$

4. Copy and complete:

a
$$\begin{array}{r} £ \\ 16·47 \\ -\ 4·06 \\ \hline \\ \hline \end{array}$$

b
$$\begin{array}{r} £ \\ 29·42 \\ -\ 13·56 \\ \hline \\ \hline \end{array}$$

c
$$\begin{array}{r} £ \\ 21·61 \\ -19·87 \\ \hline \\ \hline \end{array}$$

d
$$\begin{array}{r} £ \\ 40·60\frac{1}{2} \\ -18·87 \\ \hline \\ \hline \end{array}$$

e
$$\begin{array}{r} £ \\ 26·31 \\ -19·68\frac{1}{2} \\ \hline \\ \hline \end{array}$$

f
$$\begin{array}{r} £ \\ 47·70 \\ -28·96\frac{1}{2} \\ \hline \\ \hline \end{array}$$

Ivor Fiver and his friends

1. Answer these questions for Ivor Fiver:

   IVOR FIVER has:

Coin or note	Number
£1	2
10 p	9
5 p	2
2 p	1
1 p	7

   a How much money does he have?

   b Which items above can he afford?

   c Which of the items can he pay for exactly?

2. Answer the questions above for these people:

LLOYD BANKS

Coin or note	Number
£1	4
50 p	9
5 p	2
2 p	9
1 p	6

CLINKER COIN

Coin or note	Number
£1	1
10 p	5
5 p	4
2 p	5
1 p	10
$\frac{1}{2}$ p	6

PENNY PINCHER

Coin or note	Number
£5	1
£1	4
50 p	2
10 p	2
5 p	2
2 p	1
1 p	2

ARTHUR SIXPENCE

Coin or note	Number
£1	1
50 p	2
10 p	6
5 p	3
2 p	1
1 p	1
$\frac{1}{2}$ P	3

A square deal

Place tracing paper over this diagram. Shade over the squares which contain the answers to the questions below. How much money do you find?

£9.22	£1.79½	£14.27	£11.69	£4.68	£12.46	56½p	£1.12½	£13.71	£4.94	46½p	£11.01	£8.15½
£5.12	£2.46	£7.11½	£1.61	£9.01½	£2.10	£14.36	£14.91	£6.84	£15.44	72p	£11.51	£2.96
£7.76	£2.18	£4.50	£8.59	19p	£4.70	£7.28	£9.76	£4.16	£1.52	£2.34	£7.01	£6.74
£3.43	£2.82	£15.40	£6.94	£3.17	£0.43	£5.91	£0.01	£8.91	£1.92	76½p	£0.03	£1.38
£9.16	£14.17	£3.82½	87½p	£8.42	£3.20	81p	£3.96	£5.84	£5.09	£6.16	£1.17½	£12.58

1 $£2.15 + £7.61$

2 $£4.83 + £2.18$

3 $£6.67 + £5.79$

4 $£3.36 - £1.18$

5 $£5.16\frac{1}{2} + £9.10\frac{1}{2}$

6 $£4.16 - £3.28\frac{1}{2}$

7 $£9.18 - £8.71\frac{1}{2}$

8 $£16.16 - £11.07$

9 $£2.00 - £0.48$

10 $£2.76\frac{1}{2} + £5.82\frac{1}{2}$

11 $£10.06 - £6.10$

12 $£19.70 - £4.79$

13 $£10.00 - £5.50$

14 $£3.11 + £11.06$

15 $£0.82 + £0.87 + £0.65$

16 $£1.97 - 84\frac{1}{2}p$

17 $£6.11\frac{1}{2} - £2.29$

18 $£4.27 + £7.42$

19 $£10.00\frac{1}{2} - £5.06\frac{1}{2}$

20 $£6.99 + £4.02$

21 $£1.06 - 49\frac{1}{2}p$

22 $£2.77\frac{1}{2} - 98p$

23 $£0.64 + £0.64 + £0.64$

24 $£5.26 + £6.25$

25 $£0.97 - £0.96$

26 $28p + £1.97\frac{1}{2} + 20\frac{1}{2}p$

27 $£4.16 + £11.28$

28 $£16.62\frac{1}{2} - £9.68\frac{1}{2}$

Multiplying money

1. Copy this table and fill in the gaps.

COST

	1 packet	2 packets	3 packets	4 packets	5 packets
Beans	46 p	92 p			
Peas	$38\frac{1}{2}$ p				
Sprouts	42 p				

Problems like those above can be solved by multiplication.

3 packets of beans: £0·46 × 3

$$
\begin{array}{r}
£ \\
0 \cdot 4\,6 \\
\times \qquad 3 \\
\hline
1 \cdot 3\,8 \\
\end{array}
$$

5 packets of peas: £0·38½ × 5

$$
\begin{array}{r}
£ \\
0 \cdot 3\,8\,\tfrac{1}{2} \\
\times \qquad 5 \\
\hline
1 \cdot 9\,2\,\tfrac{1}{2} \\
\end{array}
$$

2. Set out and answer these questions:

a £1·22 × 4   b £0·36½ × 5   c £1·24½ × 3
d £2·29 × 7   e £6·61½ × 9   f £3·85 × 7
g £2·05 × 6   h £4·02½ × 8   i £21·16 × 4
j £30·06 × 5   k £2·99½ × 6   l £19·06½ × 8

Robbery!

Multiply the amount in each shape by the red figure.
Follow the correct answers, to discover which gang robbed the bank.

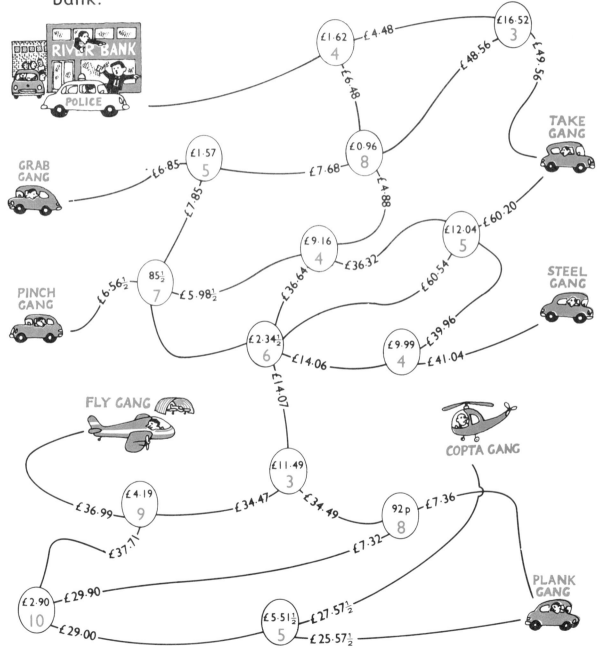

RIVER BANK
POLICE

£1.62 ④ £4.48
£6.48

£16.52 ③
£48.56
£49.56

TAKE GANG

GRAB GANG

£6.85 £1.57 ⑤
£7.85
£7.68

£0.96 ⑧
£4.88

£12.04 ⑤ £60.20
£60.54

STEEL GANG

PINCH GANG

£6.56½ 85½ ⑦
£5.98½

£9.16 ④
£36.64 £36.32

£9.99 ④ £39.96
£41.04

£2.34½ ⑥ £14.06
£14.07

FLY GANG

£11.49 ③
£34.47 £34.49

92 p ⑧ £7.36
£7.32

COPTA GANG

£4.19 ⑨
£36.99
£37.71

£2.90 ⑩ £29.90
£29.00

£5.51½ ⑤ £27.57½
£25.57½

PLANK GANG

20

Easy money

Some money problems can be made easier:

$£1.24 + 99p$ First add £1: $£1.24 + £1 = £2.24$;

then subtract 1p: $£2.24 - 1p = £2.23$

1. Write down the answers to these questions:

a $£1.78 + 99p$ b $£2.16 + 99p$ c $£3.20 + 99p$
d $£4.07 + 99p$ e $£12.23 + £1.99$ f $£16.21 + £2.99$
g $£14.20 + £0.98$ h $£2.68 + 98p$ i $£14.08 + £4.98$

$£2.28 - 99p$ First subtract £1: $£2.28 - £1 = £1.28$;

then add 1p: $£1.28 + 1p = £1.29$

2. Answer these questions:

a $£6.56 - £0.99$ b $£3.11 - 99p$ c $£12.64 - 99p$
d $£2.84 - £1.99$ e $£12.16 - £1.99$ f $£11.42 - £0.98$
g $£16.62 - £1.98$ h $£11.17 - £2.99$ i $£3.86 - £1.97$

$£0.99 \times 3 =$ $(£1 \times 3)$ $-$ $(1p \times 3)$

£3 $-$ $3p$ $=$ $£2.97$

$£4.97 \times 4 =$ $(£5 \times 4)$ $-$ $(3p \times 4)$

£20 $-$ $12p$ $=$ $£19.88$

3. Now answer these:

a $£0.99 \times 5$ b $£1.99 \times 3$ c $£4.99 \times 7$ d $£3.98 \times 6$
e $£1.98 \times 4$ f $£2.98 \times 9$ g $£10.99 \times 4$ h $£11.98 \times 8$

Eating out

Motorway Motel	
MENU	
SOUP OF THE DAY	23 p
GRAPEFRUIT	22 p
MELON	24 p
PLAICE	£1·15
SMOKED SALMON	£2·25
ROAST BEEF	£1·67
ROAST PORK	£1·46
RUMP STEAK	£2·40
STEAK PIE	£0·95
CHICKEN CASSEROLE	£1·20
HAM SALAD	£1·40
BOILED POTATOES	35 p
CHIPS	40 p
PEAS	25 p
SPROUTS	30 p
TRIFLE	45 p
ICE CREAM	40 p
TEA	20 p
COFFEE	28 p

1. How much do each of these people pay for their meal?

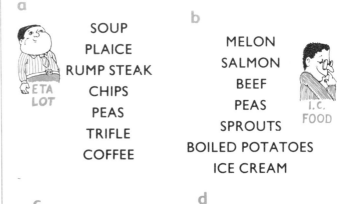

a
SOUP
PLAICE
RUMP STEAK
CHIPS
PEAS
TRIFLE
COFFEE

ETA LOT

b
MELON
SALMON
BEEF
PEAS
SPROUTS
BOILED POTATOES
ICE CREAM

I.C. FOOD

c
SOUP
MELON
HAM SALAD
CHIPS
ICE CREAM
2 CUPS OF TEA

MR CHIPS

d
GRAPEFRUIT
SALMON
CHICKEN CASSEROLE
CHIPS
SPROUTS
TRIFLE
TEA

BETTY BATTER

f
SOUP
GRAPEFRUIT
ROAST PORK
BOILED POTATOES
PEAS
TRIFLE
TEA

TOM ATO

g
MELON
PLAICE
STEAK PIE
CHIPS
SPROUTS
ICE CREAM
COFFEE

LOGAN BERRY

e
6 PLATES OF CHIPS
4 CUPS OF COFFEE

OVA WAITE

2. How much change would each person receive from a £10 note?

Check up 3

1. Work out how these costs could be paid exactly using the number of notes and coins shown:

	Cost	Notes	Coins
a	£4·26	4	6
b	£2·86	1	9
c	£3·86$\frac{1}{2}$	2	13
d	£9·62	1	7
e	£2·22	0	12
f	£15·76	4	12
g	£20·00$\frac{1}{2}$	8	1
h	£16·61	4	8

2. Answer these questions:

a £1·26 + 99p
b £3·42 − 99p
c £2·83 + £1·99
d £4·16 − £0·98
e £5·27 + £3·99
f £10·21$\frac{1}{2}$ − £0·98
g £14·20$\frac{1}{2}$ + £4·99
h £3·60 − £1·99$\frac{1}{2}$

3. CUCUMBER   LETTUCE   PEPPER

17p
23p
18p

Work out these costs:
a 2 cucumbers and 1 lettuce
b 1 lettuce and 2 peppers
c 1 cucumber and 4 peppers
d 3 lettuces and 2 peppers
e 2 cucumbers and 4 lettuces
f 6 lettuces and 4 peppers
g 1 cucumber and 8 lettuces
h 4 cucumbers and 3 lettuces

4. Copy and complete this table:

	Cost	Money given	Change
a	£2·51	£5	
b		£5	£1·82
c	£0·86$\frac{1}{2}$	£1	
d		£5	£2·64$\frac{1}{2}$
e	£1·76$\frac{1}{2}$		£0·23$\frac{1}{2}$
f		£10	£1·63
g	£8·42$\frac{1}{2}$	£10	
h	£0·07$\frac{1}{2}$	£5	

Where does all the money go?

Copy and complete these bills:

No	ITEM	Unit Cost	£
6	chickens	£1·90	£11·40
5	bags of peas	£1·07	
3	tubs of ice cream	£1·20	
4	bags of mince	£2·47	
9	bags of sprouts	£0·46½	
24	Choc ices	£0·12½	
40	Ice lollies	£0·08	
	TOTAL COST		

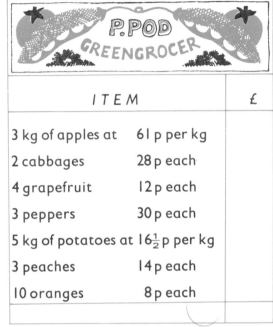

ITEM	£
3 kg of apples at 61 p per kg	
2 cabbages 28 p each	
4 grapefruit 12 p each	
3 peppers 30 p each	
5 kg of potatoes at 16½ p per kg	
3 peaches 14 p each	
10 oranges 8 p each	

No	ITEM	Unit Cost	£
3	Hammers	£1·15	
2	Screwdrivers	92½ p	
18	Hinges	1½ p	
24	Screws	1½ p	
60	Nails	½ p	
2	paintbrushes	£1·06	
3	tins paint	£4·20	
	TOTAL COST		

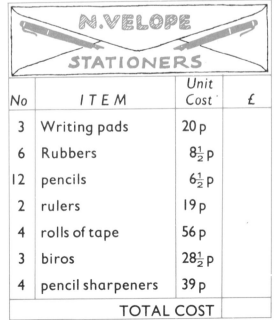

No	ITEM	Unit Cost	£
3	Writing pads	20 p	
6	Rubbers	8½ p	
12	pencils	6½ p	
2	rulers	19 p	
4	rolls of tape	56 p	
3	biros	28½ p	
4	pencil sharpeners	39 p	
	TOTAL COST		

Fair shares

5 boys share a reward of £8·45.
How much do they each receive?

DIVIDE the £8·45 into 5 equal parts:

$$
\begin{array}{r}
£ \quad\quad\quad \\
1 \cdot 6\ 9 \\
5\overline{)8\ \cdot{}^3 4 {}^4 5}
\end{array}
$$

Each share
is £1·69.

1. Copy the following and fill in the missing figures.

a
$$
\begin{array}{r}
£ \quad\quad\quad \\
0 \cdot \square\square \\
4\overline{)2 \cdot {}^2 8\ 8}
\end{array}
$$

b
$$
\begin{array}{r}
£ \quad\quad\quad \\
\square \cdot \square\square \\
5\overline{)9 \cdot {}^4 6\ {}^1 5}
\end{array}
$$

c
$$
\begin{array}{r}
£ \quad\quad\quad \\
\square \cdot 3\ \square \\
7\overline{)9 \cdot {}^\square 4\ {}^\square 5}
\end{array}
$$

d
$$
\begin{array}{r}
£ \quad\quad\quad \\
\square \cdot \square\square \\
8\overline{)4 \cdot {}^\square 2\ {}^\square 4}
\end{array}
$$

e
$$
\begin{array}{r}
£ \quad\quad\quad \\
\square \cdot \square\square \\
3\overline{)8 \cdot {}^\square 9\ {}^\square 4}
\end{array}
$$

f
$$
\begin{array}{r}
£ \quad\quad\quad \\
\square \cdot \square\square \\
6\overline{)7 \cdot {}^\square 0\ {}^\square 2}
\end{array}
$$

2. Share £6·24 equally among 4 people.

3. Share £8·54 equally among 7 people.

4. Answer the following:

a £5·48 ÷ 2   b £6·35 ÷ 5   c £4·02 ÷ 6   d £2·91 ÷ 3
e £7·60 ÷ 4   f £0·72 ÷ 9   g £8·19 ÷ 7   h £6·48 ÷ 8
i £4·80 ÷ 5   j £10·17 ÷ 9   k £18·56 ÷ 4   l £1·14 ÷ 6

Coded message

Work out this coded message and write down your answer.

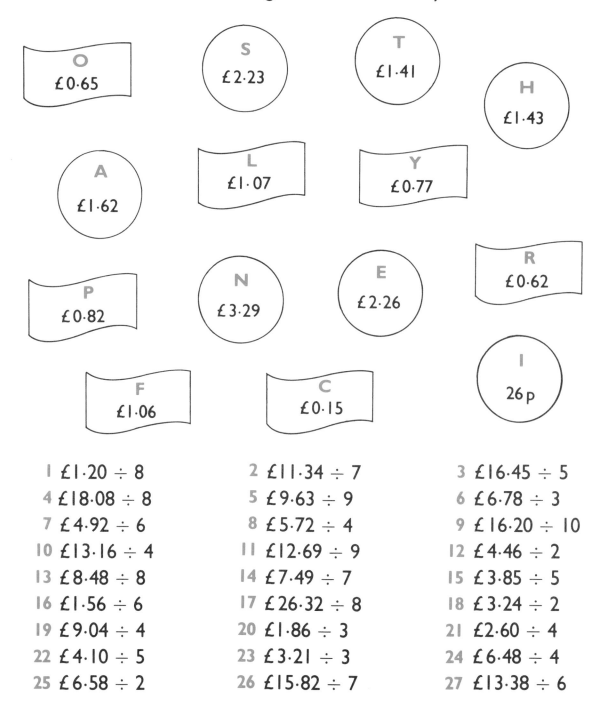

O £0·65

S £2·23

T £1·41

H £1·43

A £1·62

L £1·07

Y £0·77

P £0·82

N £3·29

E £2·26

R £0·62

I 26p

F £1·06

C £0·15

1 £1·20 ÷ 8
2 £11·34 ÷ 7
3 £16·45 ÷ 5
4 £18·08 ÷ 8
5 £9·63 ÷ 9
6 £6·78 ÷ 3
7 £4·92 ÷ 6
8 £5·72 ÷ 4
9 £16·20 ÷ 10
10 £13·16 ÷ 4
11 £12·69 ÷ 9
12 £4·46 ÷ 2
13 £8·48 ÷ 8
14 £7·49 ÷ 7
15 £3·85 ÷ 5
16 £1·56 ÷ 6
17 £26·32 ÷ 8
18 £3·24 ÷ 2
19 £9·04 ÷ 4
20 £1·86 ÷ 3
21 £2·60 ÷ 4
22 £4·10 ÷ 5
23 £3·21 ÷ 3
24 £6·48 ÷ 4
25 £6·58 ÷ 2
26 £15·82 ÷ 7
27 £13·38 ÷ 6

Flour arrangements

FLOUR – 24 p per kg   MILK – 25 p per litre
HAM – 40 p per 100 g   BREADCRUMBS – 15 p for 150 g
EGGS – 30 p for 6   SAUSAGES – £1·36 per kg
MARGARINE and LARD – 20 p per 200 g   BACON – £2·20 per kg
SAUSAGE MEAT – £1·40 per kg   MUSHROOMS – 17 p per 100 g

Work out the cost of the ingredients for the following items using the prices shown above.

HAM OMELETTE
60 g ham
2 eggs
20 g lard

SCOTCH EGGS
$\frac{1}{2}$ kg sausage meat
4 eggs
120 g breadcrumbs

FRIED BREAKFAST
(for four people)

250 g sausages
200 g bacon
4 eggs
200 g mushrooms
60 g lard

TOAD IN THE HOLE
250 g sausages
125 g flour
1 egg
$\frac{1}{10}$ litre of milk
20 g lard

SAUSAGE ROLLS
250 g sausage meat
60 g margarine
125 g flour

CAKE
125 g flour
125 g margarine
2 eggs

Box to box

Answer the questions in the first box.
If both answers are **the same** follow the **red** arrow –
but if they are **different** follow the **black** arrow.
Continue in this way as you reach each box.
What sort of box is at the end of your journey?

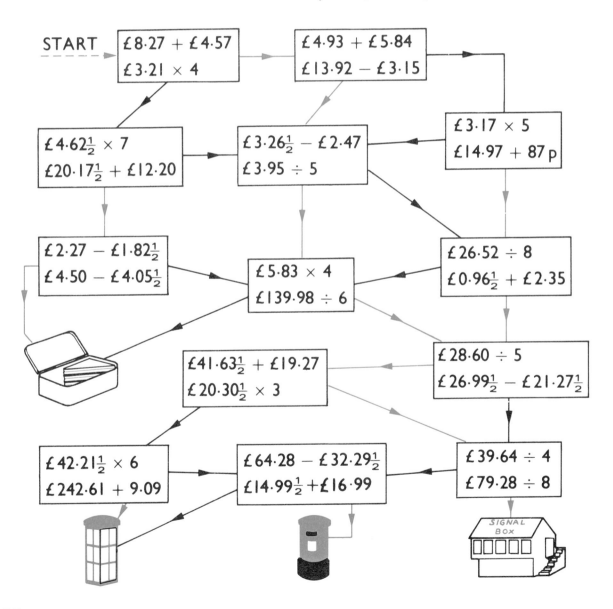

START → £8·27 + £4·57 / £3·21 × 4

£4·93 + £5·84 / £13·92 − £3·15

£3·17 × 5 / £14·97 + 87p

£4·62½ × 7 / £20·17½ + £12·20

£3·26½ − £2·47 / £3·95 ÷ 5

£2·27 − £1·82½ / £4·50 − £4·05½

£5·83 × 4 / £139·98 ÷ 6

£26·52 ÷ 8 / £0·96½ + £2·35

£41·63½ + £19·27 / £20·30½ × 3

£28·60 ÷ 5 / £26·99½ − £21·27½

£42·21½ × 6 / £242·61 + 9·09

£64·28 − £32·29½ / £14·99½ + £16·99

£39·64 ÷ 4 / £79·28 ÷ 8

SIGNAL BOX

Mixed bag

1. John wants to buy a skateboard for £23·17. He has £14·85. How much more does he need?

2. Felt pens cost 8p each. What is the cost of 32 pens?

3. Flowers cost 7p each. How many can Ann buy with a £1 note and how much change will she receive?

4. A man pays £7·60 per week towards a coat costing £91·20. How long will it take him to pay for the coat?

5. Apple pickers earn £1·68 per hour. How much do they earn in 8 hours?

6. Mrs Byalot goes shopping with £10. She spends £2·32 then £1·82$\frac{1}{2}$ then £1·09$\frac{1}{2}$. How much has she left?

7. Five oranges cost 45p. What will be the cost of 12 oranges?

Look at this example:

$$\begin{array}{r} \text{£} \\ 0\cdot 4\ 9\ \frac{1}{2} \\ 5\overline{)2\cdot{}^2 4\ {}^4 7^2\ \frac{1}{2}} \end{array}$$

Now answer these:

a £4·87$\frac{1}{2}$ ÷ 5	b £11·42$\frac{1}{2}$ ÷ 5	c £6·27$\frac{1}{2}$ ÷ 5
d £5·98$\frac{1}{2}$ ÷ 7	e £3·04$\frac{1}{2}$ ÷ 7	f £5·65$\frac{1}{2}$ ÷ 3
g £12·61$\frac{1}{2}$ ÷ 3	h £7·87$\frac{1}{2}$ ÷ 9	i £11·11$\frac{1}{2}$ ÷ 9
j £42·02$\frac{1}{2}$ ÷ 5	k £50·98$\frac{1}{2}$ ÷ 3	l £86·41$\frac{1}{2}$ ÷ 7

Crosswords 2

All the crossword answers are in pounds. When an answer is less then £1 write a '0' in front of the decimal point.

Across:

1 £2·69½ + £4·82½

5 £0·75 × 9

8 £27·61 − £18·57

9 £52·83 ÷ 9

10 £8·90 − £1·96

11 £2·69 × 3

12 £3·72½ × 8

14 £11·86½ + £21·09 + £6·96½

15 £8·52 ÷ 6

16 £107·75 ÷ 5

19 £7·81½ × 6

23 £2·89 − £0·10

25 £10·01 − £0·09

26 £6·80 ÷ 10

27 £1·89 + £2·08½ + £3·09½

28 £11·62 ÷ 7

29 £0·81½ × 4

Down:

1 £30·85 + £48·77

4 £9·95 ÷ 5

7 £14·43 × 4

16 £14·02½ + £7·98½

20 £38·97 + £30·76

24 £6·58 ÷ 7

2 £60·00 − £9·01

5 £37·94 + £27·95

13 £1·35 ÷ 9

17 £26·38 − £8·72

21 £100·00 − £10·98

3 £2·72 × 9

6 £26·03 × 3

14 £0·36 × 9

18 £119·72 ÷ 2

22 £23·19 × 4

Across:

1 £4·96 × 8

5 £5·63 × 2

7 £20·72 + £28·45

9 £5·39 × 5

Down:

2 £55·26 ÷ 6

3 £11·67 × 7

4 £28·69 + £47·58

5 £21·62½ − £7·87½

6 £3·09 × 8

8 £11·61 ÷ 9

Check up 4

1. Write answers to these:

a £9·65 ÷ 5   i £20·04 ÷ 4
b £4·86 ÷ 2   j £186·95 ÷ 5
c £16·20 ÷ 10 k £68·70 ÷ 10
d £5·67 ÷ 7   l £14·04 ÷ 6
e £17·64 ÷ 9   m £361·23 ÷ 3
f £26·48 ÷ 8   n £89·64 ÷ 9
g £41·34 ÷ 6   o £111·16 ÷ 7
h £171·60 ÷ 3 p £10·00 ÷ 8

2. Copy and complete this bill:

service-repairs-M.O.T

	£
4 Brake pads. £2·63 each	
6 Bulbs. £1·56$\frac{1}{2}$ each	
2 Wiper Blades. £3·97 each	
1 litre of oil (£3·50 per 5 litres)	
4 plugs. £1·02$\frac{1}{2}$ each	
4 car mats. £0·83$\frac{1}{2}$ each	
3 litres petrol (£0·95 per 5 litres)	
5 km tow at £0·60 per km	
20 screws. 1$\frac{1}{2}$p each	
Labour 6 hrs at £5·75 per hour	
TOTAL COST	

3. Answer the following:

a £7·52$\frac{1}{2}$ ÷ 5
b £6·52$\frac{1}{2}$ ÷ 9
c £16·90$\frac{1}{2}$ ÷ 7
d £37·66$\frac{1}{2}$ ÷ 3
e £50·08$\frac{1}{2}$ ÷ 9
f £61·21$\frac{1}{2}$ ÷ 3
g £30·76$\frac{1}{2}$ ÷ 7
h £107·62$\frac{1}{2}$ ÷ 5
i £876·29$\frac{1}{2}$ ÷ 7
j £1261·39$\frac{1}{2}$ ÷ 9

4. Write answers to these questions. Try to work out the answers in your head.

a £6·83 × 10   k £4·90 ÷ 10
b £4·72 × 10   l £6·50 ÷ 10
c £8·99 × 10   m £8·70 ÷ 10
d £6·41 × 10   n £12·40 ÷ 10
e £16·62 × 10   o £61·20 ÷ 10
f £36·27 × 10   p £36·50 ÷ 10
g £82·20 × 10   q £21·90 ÷ 10
h £70·09 × 10   r £161·60 ÷ 10
i £611·07 × 10 s £822·00 ÷ 10
j £1021·12 × 10 t £1612·80 ÷ 10

Teacher's notes   money

Whenever possible pupils should have the opportunity to handle real coins and discuss their current purchasing powers.

page 2   It is assumed that the children are familiar with the signs of '£' and 'p'.
Questions 5 and 6—it will help if the children can handle real coins whilst answering these questions.

3   Real coins should be available if possible.

4   "Basher" has the most money.

6   Knowledge of the term '$\frac{1}{100}$' is assumed. Children should already be familiar with the amounts of money shown as decimal fractions.

7   The exit is "door B".

9   Practice with real coins will be most helpful.

10   The holiday is in Brighton.

11   Teachers should stress the importance of setting out the bills accurately.

13   Teachers should ensure that children thoroughly understand all parts of the examples.

14   Shopping spree: Mr. Bone £3.42; Mrs. Buss £4.66; Bill Ding £2.82; Bagsov Cash £7.64; Bob Bee £5.00; Jim Shuze £5.75; Joe Kerr £3.50.

18   The hidden money is 50p.

19   Experience of multiplication is essential.

20   The bank was robbed by the "Copta Gang".

25   Experience of division is assumed.

26   The coded message is "Can elephants fly in aeroplanes".

28   The telephone box.